MICHEL GAGNON

My True Story

"How I acquired and invested in Real estate"

This book was professionally typeset on Reedsy.
Find out more at reedsy.com

Contents

INTRODUCTION

My name is Michel Gagnon, I am 48 years old and I am a French Canadian living in a small town in the province of Quebec, Canada. I started investing in real estate about ten years ago.

I wanted to write a book on how I got started as a real estate investor and tell you about the steps I took to encourage people who have not yet taken the leap into real estate investing.

At the time, I had no idea that investing in real estate would be so easy. Despite the few properties I own, my investments have, to this day, secured my first millions. But a million today is not that important when you think about it.

I don't think it's important to be the biggest or the richest, but the most profitable. It's not about the number of properties, it's about having a great return and being comfortable with the number of properties you have.

I know people who have a lot of real estate, but who are not very profitable, as they have not had the time to develop their investor mentality to profit from it. So this book is for first-time investors, those who have not yet taken the leap into real estate.

If you are already an investor, you will understand everything I am going to say here and it will only stimulate your desire to invest. I will try to keep it simple: no numbers, no percentages, no ratios. I will simply offer you the necessary motivation to make your first real estate investments and share my personal story with you.

It is important to understand that real estate is fundamentally a state of mind, a *mindset*. You must be curious about everything that revolves around:

- finance;
- personal budget;
- Money (knowing how money works in general);
- and all the other subjects that concern money.

Because real estate is all about that. As for me, I grew up in a small town in Quebec, Canada, where my father was a contractor. I had a great childhood. Back in the day, I didn't take care of my personal finances and I wasn't interested in money matters. I thought that all I had to do was work to make money and that everything made sense. I spent everything I earned.

My first real thought about money was when I got a rewarding job, with the Canadian government, and started earning a good salary. At that point, I asked myself, *"How can I take this money and give as little of it back to the government in taxes and just grow it?"* I wasn't thinking about real estate investing yet, but I knew one thing: I had to get my personal finances in order.

I still had loans and credit card debt from when I wasn't making much money. I had the idea that if I wanted to invest in real estate, I needed to have healthy, balanced personal finances. At that time, I didn't invest much as my priority was to simply get my personal finances in order.

I started to pay off my student loans and pay off my remaining credit card debts, to then start putting some savings aside. And it worked! In this book, I don't have a miracle recipe, my ultimate goal is to help you take your first steps in *real estate* . You must think real estate and act as a real estate investor. If I can get you to do that during this reading, I will have achieved my goal.

We're going to talk about a variety of topics: how I bought my first building and where I got the money for it. This question comes up a lot. There is one thing I can tell you already: I read a lot of books to develop my real estate *mindset* to find my first dollar to buy my first building. Again, ten years ago, I had no intention of investing in real estate.

"Why did I invest?" you might ask… The answer is that I realized that the most logical thing for me to do was to become a real estate investor; that this was how I could keep the most money for myself and give the least amount back to the government. This is by taking advantage of being able to grow my money in real estate investing.

The Canadian and U.S. financial systems are unique and you need to understand how both work. Then you'll find that investing in real estate makes sense. A lot of sense.

I don't want you to think this is easy, but the *mindset* you develop will do the work for you as you go along. Obviously, this won't happen just by reading this book, but I'm convinced I will motivate you to grow it in the future.

A lot of people ask me about real estate investing, but I find that very few actually make the move. That's the main problem. I think that's a shame and I'm going to try to unblock your mindset.

So, keep in mind, during this reading, that it is your real estate investor *mindset* that should guide and motivate you. Afterwards, the rest will follow, as it did for me.

Enjoy your reading, Michel

FIRST STEP BEFORE INVESTING IN REAL ESTATE

GET YOUR PERSONAL FINANCES IN ORDER

I f you attend conferences or seminars on *"how to invest in real estate"*, many speakers will tell you that you don't need money to invest. This is partly true, because my first purchase was made without any personal savings…

I'll tell you more about that later. However, I believe that your financial situation must still be clear. You need to have a stable job and, if possible, a good salary. If you need to get a second job so you can get a better salary and get your personal finances in order faster, do it.

It also means that building your budget is essential. For me, doing my financial review every quarter stimulates me and allows me to see how my real estate is doing. Spending less, budgeting and earning more will advance your mindset and lead you to having a real estate investor *mindset.* Otherwise, personally, I think it will be difficult for you.

Of course, you can always find success stories on the internet, but that's not my case and I believe that many successful investors will tell you the same thing. First and foremost, you need to improve your credit score, reduce the number of credit cards you have, reduce your use of loans, etc. Clean up your finances and, if necessary, list the financial institutions that can help you do this better.

Be careful, some will want to lend you more money while others will want to help you. Go around the banks, don't hesitate to take time for this, reduce your debts little by little.

I know that some people will tell you to liquidate your debts in one go, from the smallest to the largest, to motivate you, and this is a good method. However, for me, I have reduced my debts overall, but a little bit at a time overall. But it doesn't matter how you do the process; what matters is that you get rid of them in the end.

One way or another, get your finances in order. If you haven't already done so, this is my first recommendation.

Read and be informed

You need to know how money works in general. If you don't know how much you pay per month for your cell phone, internet connection or anything else, you need to find out. Knowing how much interest you pay on your loans is also very important to develop your *mindset.*

Personally, it allows me to motivate myself to calculate how much more capital I can put into my investments and it increases my *mindset.*

Indeed, calculating a loan with 1% more or less makes us understand very quickly the power of compound interest. Keeping track of your credit score history is, in my opinion, a good start. Some will tell you that there are people who work in this field to keep you informed of all this and I agree. But for myself, I try to keep up with my credit report rates and my credit score alone. Also reading all the publications (like this book) opens up your *mindset* and motivates your sense of investing.

As far as I am concerned, I have read several publications. All these publications have opened my mind. Several channels on the web also talk about different subjects and are very informative. Recently, I was listening to a program on real estate acquisition in the metaverse.

Interesting! This is possibly what I think will happen in the future, although for now it is not very clear to me.

Being part of a real estate investor's club is also a good way to go. Personally, I used to attend the meetings of these clubs, simply to get information and not to get training. I think the costs are too high. In my opinion, it is the first steps that are difficult to take and not the knowledge to acquire. Many good (serious) websites can give you more than enough information to give you an excellent starting toolbox. With professionals to guide you, real estate investing is very accessible. There is no need to spend tons of money to take courses. That's my personal opinion.

Finding money to buy my first property

I bought my first property with the help of my father. This is called *love money*, which means using other people's money to invest in a first property. I think this is the only logical and intelligent way to make your first real estate purchase in the short and medium term. However, you won't be able to convince one of your relatives without having an investor mentality and having shaky personal finances and without sufficient income.

If you work two jobs, have a good salary, and have a balanced budget, people will be more open and confident to lend you money. When I approached my father to make my first purchase, I was faced with a person who had not developed a real estate investor mindset. My father had a good entrepreneurial *mindset*, but different from real estate.

I managed to convince him by making the numbers speak for themselves. As you read on and increase your knowledge of real estate investing, you will realize that many things happen at once when you invest (capitalization, capital gains, income, tax reduction, etc.) and all of this, simply by receiving rental income.

You're going to tell me that there's tenant management. Yes, of course, but first you have to make the numbers talk. Only then will you realize that your tenants' well-being will become your priority, because tenant management will be directly linked to your numbers. It's automatic; you don't have to worry about tenant management.

Personally, I have great tenants and I think they have a great landlord. Every holiday season, I send a small gift and, on several occasions, some of them tell me they never received such a gift from their previous landlord. It means a lot to me. I have three tenants in my buildings who were there even before I bought them over ten years ago…

Mindset to have to find my first financial support

Your *mindset* is a set of beliefs that shape how you make sense of the world and yourself. It influences how you think, feel, and behave.

When I approached my father to help me with the initial down payment, I thought about asking for an inheritance before he passed away. You're going to tell me that this is very morbid, disrespectful, etc. Maybe, but many very rich people do it.

My father had accumulated a certain retirement portfolio and, according to my calculations, if he loaned me a down payment, I could either ask to receive an inheritance now or borrow some money from him.

Finally, my father gave me a gift. Showing him the positives and negatives (which are less important than the positives) of real estate investing made him realize that this gift was going to be used wisely. Ask him today what he thinks about it .

I am sure you can also find someone you know (aunt, uncle, etc) who has accumulated a considerable amount of money. If you do your calculations the right way and have your personal finances in order, then it will be possible to borrow a certain amount of money to make your first purchase with a reasonable interest rate, for you and for the person lending you the money. Do the math.

When I talked about inheritance above, I was also talking about family wealth. The investment I made will remain in the family after my death for my partner, my nephews, etc. So, nothing is lost in the end and making my father understand this was the same as making him understand that an inheritance, a gift or anything else was not going to be lost in the future of the family estate.

I often think that when I die, my nephews will be able to receive the income from the real estate investments I made in the past. Over time, the buildings will have increased in value and the loans associated with those buildings will be minimal. I am proud to leave them this.

FIVE MISTAKES NOT TO MAKE

DO NOT LISTEN TO OTHER PEOPLE'S OPINIONS

If I can give one good piece of advice, it is to *not listen* to other people's opinions. You need to form a real estate *mindset* and move forward with what you have. I sometimes have conversations with some people who tell me they hate tenants and rental properties. This leads to them having virtually no money saved and living month to month, like most of the population.

Canadians' and Americans' population finances are very problematic. So, if the majority of the population is having trouble managing their finances, why listen to them?

Personally, I listen to web channels about real estate, but not all of them are interesting. However, this exercise allows me to develop my critical *mindset* on the subject and allows me to question myself on certain points to improve my understanding or simply to understand certain particularities that still escape me.

Avoid listening to success stories, stories like the one I am writing are probably more common. Instant or short-term success may surely be possible, but I doubt it will be sustainable for the future. This is my opinion.

Thinking about the future

L iving one day at a time is good. However, if I don't think about the future, I will never invest in real estate. Also, we are only passing through this earth (if you didn't know that yet), so forget about limits! Go for it now, because tomorrow it might be too late.

When I talked about inheritance earlier, this is part of my *mindset*. Real estate acquisition will continue after you are gone. Have professionals around you to plan your estate after your death to avoid family conflicts.

Many people make acquisitions but upon their death, inheritance issues emerge. Make a will, draw up and sign clear agreements with your partners (if it is the case). Keep all your records in order, which is also very important for good management.

Don't wait until you have the necessary down payment for your purchase

As I mentioned in the first part, I used my father's money to make my first purchase. Otherwise, I would have probably bought real estate, but much later. If you know the power of compound interest, you know that investing should be done as early as possible so that you can have good rental income and very low loans on your properties when you retire. Future financial freedom is also one of my priorities, which is to live off my investments when I retire.

Often when people tell me they don't have the money to invest in real estate, I remind them that they can go into it with other people, friends, family or whatever. Many people will tell you that this is not recommended, even dangerous, but I believe that it is better to have a 5-10-20-30 or 40% share in an investment with someone helping you than 0%.

With good professionally drafted partnership documents, it will always be possible to resell your shares in the future.

If the rental income has been managed properly, it will be very easy to resell one's shares in the future, or to buy out others' shares if your *mindset* has developed well. Moreover, with the increase in real estate prices in recent years, even if resale is not possible, it will surely be relevant to refinance this portion to invest in another property.

Personally, I have never done a partnership, but ask a professional if you are interested.

Surround yourself with competent people

Don't get into real estate investing without professional help. Personally, I have dealt with professionals in the financial field to clarify whether my interpretations were correct.

Finance is a special field. Remember to have your calculations validated and your understanding of returns clarified. Have your tax forms and all other business documents done by professionals. My father often advised me to avoid these expenses, which he considered unnecessary. However, my real estate *mindset* told me not to skimp on these expenses to avoid the pitfalls. This was a very good approach in my opinion.

Plus, it's part of my building's operating costs. Hire good, reputable contractors with good references. Today, we hear horror stories of people who have had renovations done with disreputable contractors.

Personally, I try to get an opinion from a friend or former colleague to see if this company is recommendable. Get good paperwork done if you are associated with partners. For my father's donation mentioned earlier, we did it all formally. Not because there was no mutual trust, but to make it official if something happened to me or my dad.

Manage your budget from a single account

Personally, I manage my personal finances separately from my real estate finances. This creates a better tracking and overview, separate from my real estate and personal receipts and payments. Today, everything is done by electronic transfer, electronic payment to the supplier and all this becomes very difficult to follow.

I manage my real estate finances from one financial institution and my personal finances from a separate financial institution. In addition to keeping track of my transactions with ease, this allows me to compare the two financial institutions when renewing my loans to get the best deals.

The world of financial institutions is very interesting and particular and I like to understand how they work in order to use them to my advantage when renewing my home loans.

Don't be embarrassed to renegotiate your loans and not take the first offers you get. Financial institutions are companies and are always trying to make the most money.

Personally, I try to deal with financial institutions that have a large real estate portfolio. Some institutions are simply not qualified to recommend the right financial products for real estate and that's why I deal with an institution that is known to be very solid in real estate.

I also try to find financial advisors who invest in real estate themselves. Someone who owns real estate has a similar *mindset* to me and we can have interesting discussions since we speak the same language. Also, they often know the local market so we can have conversations about occupancy rates and financial products to deal in.

FIVE ESSENTIAL THINGS TO KNOW

HAVE A GOOD LIFE ETHIC

Your state of mind goes with your personal well-being. Real estate acquisition brings material wealth, but it does not bring happiness and joy, although it contributes to it. Work to have good relationships. Keeping the same person by my side for more than 24 years has allowed me to be successful as a real estate investor. The fact that my partner hates real estate keeps my happiness rational positive.

It includes investment, but does not include management. Two completely different things, but they go hand in hand. Couple relationships are complicated, but like real estate investing, you have to learn and work on that facet like I do with real estate.

Have a healthy lifestyle. Regular exercise keeps my mind free and available for a new openness. The body is like the *mindset*, it needs exercise. A good diet, enough sleep is something we think is easy, but with today's hectic lifestyle, with electronics and such where everything is fast paced, it is not always obvious, and we need to work on that as well.

Prioritize your choices

Personally, when I have a decision to make, I prioritize my choices. Always with an eye on what is best and what is best now. As I said before, life is a struggle and tomorrow is another day. Do what's best for now.

Without letting myself be carried away by the desire or the emotion, I prioritize the *now* and *right away*. As an example, in my life, I had to do several jobs on my personal house. However, some jobs were more important than others, so I had to prioritize. My basic idea was this, *"If I were to die tomorrow, what would be the most important thing to do on the house so that my significant other would not have that burden to bear in the future?"* I always have the *mindset* to go for it today, one day at a time and tomorrow is another day.

Personally, I draw two columns entitled "advantages/disadvantages". All decisions are important, but they all have advantages and disadvantages. Some expenses have more benefits than others. When I take the time to look at the paper, I see exactly where these expenses fit in with my other priorities. Then I talk to my financial advisors, my partner or anyone else I really trust to confirm that my priorities are right. Quite simply.

Spend less

Personally, I'm still working on applying this concept. I spend way too much. The only good thing is that I recognize this and am still working on it. When I find that I am spending too much, I send an amount directly to a separate savings account in an automated way. Just so I don't have easy access to it and make sure I have to take an action (the action of making the transfer) to access it.

So, set your budget, try to make more money and spend less. When you do your first review in three months, you'll see how money is a tool that works for us when it's managed well.

Decrease the Number of Times You're in a Store. Grocery shopping every other week instead of weekly will decrease your food bill. In fact, decreasing the number of times you enter a store, in general, will guarantee you spend less this year than last year.

Audit One habit at a Time. Trying to change all of your habits a once is a recipe for misery. Instead, just take one habit at a time and figure out how to get what you WANT, while spending less on it.

But before we dive into the strategies, you've got to calculate your benchmark so that you know when you're spending less than last year, *and when you're not.*

Set aside a minimum of 10% when you come into money

Regardless of whether you have a large income or not, I recommend that you put 10% of all your savings in a separate account. Sure, you can put in 5%, 10% or 20%, but start with 10% for the next six months and work your way up from there. Putting money aside will not buy you real estate in the short or medium term, but it will allow you to see how money works and help you develop *your* investment *mindset.*

With the money you saved in those six months, buy something that will last. For me, it was the purchase of an ounce of gold, quite simply? Because gold is a precious material that shows wealth. When I look at my ounce of gold, I dream of becoming a better real estate investor and it motivates me.

Every day I watch the value of this single ounce of gold rise and it is part of the health of my *mindset*. This gold coin is inert, serving no purpose and sitting on my desk. However, this meaning shows that putting that 10% aside allows me to acquire that thing that I physically own.

When I look at this ounce, I wonder how to make more sacrifices to get even more, as I do with my future real estate plans. It's all in the *mindset*, as I've been saying all along.

If you don't think you can put 10% aside, schedule an automatic transfer every time your paycheck comes in. That way, when you go to your bank account, your 10% won't show up. When you look at your budget and balance sheet, you may find that this small periodic amount is growing. And it will be yours and yours alone.

Respect

As I have said from the beginning, we are only passing through this earth. So are the people around us. We must respect others and understand their reality. I am an empathetic and emotional person. However, I don't get carried away with the difficulties of my tenants when they are in trouble.

Respect comes when the other person respects us, it is not a one-way street. When two respectful people come together, anything is possible. My tenants understand the sacrifices I have had to make to acquire and keep my buildings and respect that.

When there is a rent increase, they understand very well the reality of rising costs of living; otherwise, we start discussing about it.

In my last ten years, I have only had two difficult tenants out of my total tenants. That's very few. The *mindset of* respect is essential before investing in real estate.

If you want to buy real estate, simply to make income, good luck... . You'll probably succeed, but your work ethic will be broken, as mentioned in my number 1 point of essential things to know in this first part.

There is also respect for the contractors and professionals we work with, which includes fair and equitable compensation. Many of them try to get the lowest price, but the quality of the contractors at low prices can make you wonder.

If you are familiar with money, finance, pricing, etc., you can understand how much a contractor costs at the right price, who gives you a guarantee on his work; who works fast and well and with quality products. If a contractor gives you a good price, he will automatically have to cut back on other elements: the quality of the products, the experience of his employees or anything else.

I believe I pay my contractors the right price. As a result, when I need their services, they make themselves available quickly. If I were disrespectful and always trying to cut a dollar in half, they probably wouldn't be as interested in coming to work for me.

When I talked about surrounding yourself with competent people, it has a cost. And I believe that you can't have one without the other.

Conclusion

To conclude, this book is not meant to be a miracle recipe book to real estate success. It is simply a snapshot at a given time, of a person like me, that explains how I was able to invest in real estate.

As I mentioned in the book, *mindset* is the key to success that will make you successful. You need to train and develop your *mindset* and respect life and the people around you by having a good life ethic and I am confident that you will be able to succeed.

Success is not measured by the number of apartments you have, but by what you are able to accomplish. That's it! If for me, it's being where I am today, the goal is achieved.

Oh, yes. I forgot to tell you that my first building allowed me to acquire my second building, with the accumulated profits from the first. So yes, there is such a thing as making your second acquisition with the help of your first acquisition.

The goal today is to motivate you to get started and take the first steps in real estate. Thank you for reading and good luck in your future investments.

www.ingramcontent.com/pod-product-compliance
Lightning Source LLC
Chambersburg PA
CBHW060926130726
48001CB00006B/2447